Class No.

Leab
(M

Loan per

A fine o
part of
ove

The Making of a Champion

A World-Class Sprinter

Clive Gifford

www.heinemann.co.uk/library

Visit our website to find out more information about **Heinemann Library** books.

To order:

☎ Phone 44 (0) 1865 888066

🖹 Send a fax to 44 (0) 1865 314091

🖥 Visit the Heinemann Bookshop at www.heinemann.co.uk/library to browse our catalogue and order online.

First published in Great Britain by Heinemann Library, Halley Court, Jordan Hill, Oxford OX2 8EJ, part of Harcourt Education. Heinemann is a registered trademark of Harcourt Education Ltd.

Editorial: Andrew Farrow and Dan Nunn
Design: David Poole and Geoff Ward
Illustrations: Geoff Ward
Picture Research: Rebecca Sodergren and Fiona Orbell
Production: Viv Hichens

Originated by Ambassador Litho Ltd
Printed in China by WKT Company Limited

ISBN 0 431 18921 8
08 07 06 05
10 9 8 7 6 5 4 3 2

British Library Cataloguing in Publication Data

Gifford, Clive
  A World-Class Sprinter - (The Making of a Champion)
  1. Sprinting - Juvenile literature
  2. Sprinting - Training - Juvenile literature
  I. Title
  796.4'22
A full catalogue record for this book is available from the British Library.

Acknowledgements

The publishers would like to thank the following for permission to reproduce photographs:

Action Plus pp. **6 top** (Richard Francis), **11 bottom** (Neil Tingle), **12 top** (Gary Kirk), **16 top, 18 top** (Gary Kirk), **24 top** (DPPI/Millereau), **25** (DPPI/Millereau); Corbis pp. **14–15 bottom, 19 bottom** (Bettman), **19 top** (Wally McNamee), **29 bottom** (Duomo), **33 bottom** (Bettman), **35 bottom** (Duomo), **38** (S. Carmona), **40** (Sygma/Pasquini Cedric); David Hoffman Photo Library p. **32**; Empics pp. **5 bottom** (Topham Picturepoint), **17, 20** (Adam Davy), **26** (Mike Egerton), **27 bottom, 35 top** (Steve Mitchell), **42** (Steve Mitchell), **43** (Steve Mitchell); Getty Images pp. **5 top** (Michael Steele), **6 bottom** (Allsport UK), **7** (Allsport UK), **9 bottom** (Allsport UK), **15 top** (Allsport/Clive Mason), **21 bottom, 22, 23 bottom, 24 bottom, 37** (Allsport/IOC Olympic Museum); Liz Eddison p. **28**; PA Photos/EPA pp. **9 top, 31 bottom**; Popperfoto p. **36**; Reuters pp. **4** (Andy Clark), **8** (Chris Helgren), **10** (STR), **11 middle** (Gary Hershorn), **12 bottom** (Eric Gallard), **21 top** (HO), **29 top** (Gary Hershorn), **30** (Ian Hodgson), **31 top** (Michael Leckel), **33 top** (Will Burgess), **39** (Sergio Perez), **41** (Zanil Abd Halim); Science Photo Library p. **27 top** (Mauro Fermariello); Swift Performance Equipment p. **34**.

Cover photograph reproduced with permission of Empics Sports Photo Agency/Neal Simpson.

Every effort has been made to contact copyright holders of any material reproduced in this book. Any omissions will be rectified in subsequent printings if notice is given to the publishers.

Contents

Words printed in bold letters, **like these**, are explained in the Glossary.

Introducing sprinting

Few things in athletics can compete with the tension and excitement of the final of a 100m or 200m sprint at the Olympics. Absolute silence greets the sprinters as they get onto their **starting blocks** and wait for the starter's gun. As the gun fires, the sprinters explode out of their blocks and the crowd erupts. Ten or twenty seconds of drama later, the race is over. The new Olympic champion can begin their lap of honour.

Elite athletes with a disability also take part in major international sprinting competitions. Nigerian Adekunle Adesoji broke the world record for the 100m for blind athletes at the 2002 Commonwealth Games, with a time of 10.76 seconds.

The ultimate dream

Champion sprinters are the fastest men and women on Earth, reaching speeds of over 40 kph during a race. For top sprinters, winning the 100m and 200m races at the World Championships, and especially the Olympics, are lifelong goals. US sprinter Maurice Greene won the 100m gold at the 2000 Olympics in Sydney, Australia. 'I did the job I came to do and it was something I have been dreaming of since I was a child,' he said afterwards.

Glamour, hard work and sacrifice

Around the world, sprinters are amongst the most famous participants in athletics. Their events may only last a few short seconds, but the races live long in spectators' memories.

Sprinting at big athletics events may appear glamorous, but away from the big stadia there are months and months of tough training and sacrifice. As one star sprinter once said, 'The hardest thing a sprinter has to put up with is knowing you train all year just to run nine seconds.'

A sprinter's physique

Although sprinters tend to have a similar **physique**, with a muscular upper body and relatively long legs, sprinters do actually vary in size. British sprinter, Linford Christie, the 1992 Olympic 100m champion, was very muscular and stood 1.9m tall. US sprinter, Maurice Greene, is shorter at 1.7m. A sprinter's physique is the result of years of hard training. That, along with a good diet, excellent coaching and a huge amount of dedication and belief gives them a chance of becoming an Olympic champion.

Tim Montgomery, who was later involved in a drugs controversy, poses in front of his 2002 world record time.

Wilma Rudolph

Many sprinters have overcome great challenges and difficulties to become the best. One such sprinter was US athlete Wilma Rudolph. She was born with polio and contracted pneumonia and scarlet fever as a young child. Doctors told her that she would never be able to walk properly. Rudolph showed great determination to not only walk but to run – and run incredibly fast. She was the first woman to run the 200m in under 23 seconds and won gold medals in the 100m, 200m and 4 x 100m relay at the 1960 Olympics.

Starting young

Sprinting is open to competitors of all ages, and many of today's top sprinters started running as young children. Others came to sprinting relatively late in their mid- or late-teenage years. With enough talent, dedication and good coaching, both early and late starters can progress and succeed.

Many glittering sprint careers have started at a school sports day. A number of top sprinters have recalled how they wanted to win every race they ran as schoolchildren.

A winning start

Most sprint stars can remember their first race and their first victory. The US Olympic 100m gold medallist Maurice Greene, for example, was eight years old when he entered three races for children a year older than he was and won them all. The feeling of beating the other competitors and winning is an enjoyable and addictive experience.

In 1999, the first World Youth Championships (for ages fifteen to seventeen) were held, at Bydgoszcz in Poland. The winner of the men's 100m final was British sprinter, Mark Lewis-Francis (pictured right).

Moving up the levels

Being the fastest child in a school year is only the start. Schools in all countries send their best young athletes to local schools' sports meetings. The very best performers from these competitions may compete at regional events that group competitors together by age. Countries like the USA, Australia and the UK have large numbers of athletics clubs and most of these have junior sections. Australian star Cathy Freeman, for example, joined her local athletics club at the age of eleven. National junior athletics championships are usually targeted at older children, above the age of fourteen, although this varies from country to country.

Early inspiration

Many top sprinters can recall a moment or event that led to them becoming hooked on sprinting. For US Olympic 100m gold medallist Marion Jones, it was the arrival of the Olympics in her home town of Los Angeles in 1984. After watching some of the events on television, she ran into her room and wrote: 'I want to be an Olympic champion.'

Late starters

A number of top sprinters played a range of sports and did not focus on sprinting until they were in their late teens. Namibian Olympic silver medallist Frankie Fredericks was a keen football player, as was Trinidad's Ato Boldon. Growing up in Trinidad, Boldon did not receive his first serious coaching and training until he was sixteen years old.

Cathy Freeman

Cathy Freeman's family was poor but determined to give her the chance of fulfilling her sprinting potential. Her stepfather travelled long distances raising money and the family planned their holidays around state and national junior championships. In 1989, at the age of fifteen, Freeman ran the 100m in 11.67 seconds, a fast time for her age. Her school coach put her forward for Olympic **trials** and a year later, Freeman was part of the Australian 4 x 100m relay team that won gold at the 1990 **Commonwealth Games**.

Coaching

Young sprinters often rely on their raw talent and speed without giving too much thought to training or technique. Sprinters must improve technically if they are to progress to the top of sprinting, and all champion sprinters turn to coaches to get the very best out of their bodies and their abilities.

What a coach provides

Coaches provide assistance in all sorts of areas. For example, Maurice Greene's coach, John Smith, worked with Greene on his starting technique to make him one of the sharpest starters in world sprinting. Coaches advise on all aspects of a sprinter's technique, from driving out of the **starting blocks** to keeping relaxed in the last stages of a race.

Coaches assess a sprinter's running style in great detail. Through technical coaching and training, coaches get sprinters to make adjustments to their body position, arm movements or stride length. Coaches also devise training plans and systems to increase a sprinter's flexibility, speed, strength and **stamina**.

Part of a team

A champion sprinter's coach is often part of a team of people all seeking to get the best performance possible out of an athlete. Coaches work with specialists in diet and nutrition to see that the sprinter eats and drinks well (see pages 28–29). They also work with doctors, **physiotherapists** and other medical staff to help their athlete recover from illness or injury.

Some of sprinting's top coaches work with a number of athletes in a training group. American John Smith (pictured here) has coached Cathy Freeman and Jon Drummond and was both Maurice Greene and Ato Boldon's coach when they finished first and second respectively in the 100m final of the 2000 Olympics.

A close relationship

Top coaches and sprinters work incredibly closely together and spend many hours in each other's company. Over time, a sprinter's coach can become more than their chief technical advisor about running technique and training plans. They can become a confidant and father or mother figure to a sprinter. Many top sprinters become close friends with their coaches and a large number stay with the same coach throughout their sprinting careers.

Taking coaching seriously

Although US star Michael Johnson ran throughout his teenage years, he left high school without winning any major events. It was Baylor University's head athletics coach, Clyde Hart, who recognized something special in Johnson and offered him a scholarship. Hart urged Johnson to take training and running seriously and showed him ways to improve his starting and his running technique. Johnson later triumphed at the Olympics as well as smashing the 200m world record. Hart remained as Johnson's coach throughout the runner's illustrious career.

Trinidad's Ato Boldon only began to receive serious coaching in 1989 and 1990, yet in 1992 he won both the 100m and 200m gold at the World Junior Championships (for athletes under the age of 20) in Seoul, South Korea.

Sprinting equipment

Sprinters do not need much specialist equipment, but the few pieces of equipment they do use are extremely important. Top sprinters often have their equipment especially made to fit them. They also follow research into clothing and footwear very carefully. Anything that might help them run faster, even if it just knocked a hundredth of a second off their time, could make all the difference between winning gold, silver or bronze – or not winning anything at all!

US sprinter Marion Jones coasts home in 2000 to win a 100m race in 10.93 seconds. It was the first outing for her new all-in-one Swift Suit made by the sportswear company, Nike.

Keeping warm

Sprinters take special care to keep warm in the period before a race. Keeping warm allows their muscles to stay flexible, which reduces the chances of a muscle strain or injury. Sprinters only remove their warm-up tracksuit tops and bottoms shortly before they complete their final stretching exercises and head to the **starting blocks**. It is equally important to keep warm during training, especially in cold winter conditions.

Beneath their tracksuits, sprinters' racewear tends to be close-fitting and until the 1990s consisted of thin vests or tops tucked into lightweight shorts. More recently, many sprinters have opted for all-in-one bodysuits like the one worn above by US sprinter Marion Jones. These are made of stretchy fabrics that create less friction through the air as the sprinters run.

A sprinter's spikes

Top sprinters have a number of pairs of high-quality training shoes for different tasks such as outdoor work and weight training. The shoes that they wear for racing are quite different to ordinary trainers or sneakers. They tend to be extremely light (as little as 130g compared to over 400g for many ordinary training shoes) and they are extremely flexible at the front. Sprinters run on the balls of their feet, so the front part of the soles have short, sharp spikes which help provide grip.

Marion Jones laces up her spiked racing shoes. The spikes are designed to provide enough grip for the sprinter to drive forward but without slowing them down by generating too much friction.

Starting equipment: then and now

American sprint legend Jesse Owens won his 1936 Olympic sprinting races using small holes dug into the cinder track to give his feet grip as he pushed off to start running. Today's top sprint competitions insist on sprinters using standardized starting blocks. These support the sprinter's feet and increase the power the sprinter can obtain from a crouch start.

Flying starts

The difference between success and failure in an Olympic sprint final can often be measured in hundredths of a second. A sprinter who gets an excellent start may find themselves ahead of their rivals. With 100m and 200m races being over so quickly, athletes who make a poor start have little chance of recovering.

False starts

Sprinters want to react quickly to the starter's gun, be off their **starting blocks** and into the race as soon as possible. But trying to anticipate the starting gun and gain an unfair advantage is called a false start. If a sprinter starts before the gun has been fired or has a **reaction time** of under 0.12 of a second after the gun, then they are considered to have made a false start. The starter fires their pistol a second time to tell the sprinters to return to their blocks for a restart.

An athlete drives out of her blocks in a 100m race before the starter's pistol has fired. Her false start is noted and communicated by track officials, and the race has to be restarted.

Female sprinters in a 60m World Indoor Championships semi-final explode out of their starting blocks. The winner of the final crossed the line in just 7.06 seconds.

Measuring reaction time

Since the early 1990s, reaction times off the starting blocks have been measured electronically to judge whether an athlete has made a false start. Electronic sensors are fitted to the starting blocks and linked to both a computer and the starter's gun. These sensors measure the pressure of the sprinter's feet on the blocks. An increase in pressure followed by a rapid decrease shows the sprinter driving away off the blocks. The computer and sensors work together to measure the sprinter's reaction time to the starting pistol.

Disqualification

For many years, a sprinter was **disqualified** if he or she made two false starts in a race. At the start of 2003 the rule was changed. Now, only one false start per race is allowed before a second false start by any athlete sees them disqualified and removed from the race.

Starting style

All sprinters have their own starting style, but a typical method is illustrated below:

1) On the starter's order of 'On your marks', each sprinter gets into their starting blocks with their arms straight but not locked at the elbow joint.

2) On the order of 'Set', the sprinter adopts their starting position with their hips positioned higher than their shoulders.

3) As the starting gun fires, the sprinter's hands leave the ground, the front leg drives hard against the block whilst the rear leg comes through to take the first forward stride.

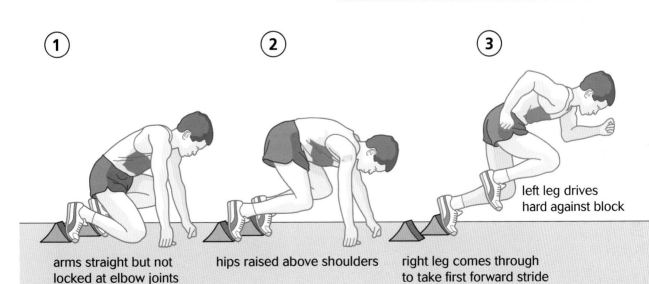

① arms straight but not locked at elbow joints

② hips raised above shoulders

③ right leg comes through to take first forward stride

left leg drives hard against block

Reaching top speed

As the starter's gun fires, sprinters need to react rapidly to power off their **starting blocks** and start racing. In the first few strides, sprinters must match their explosive power with balance, coordination and control in order to reach top speed.

Driving out of the blocks

Sprinters leave their blocks by driving hard with their front leg against the block while pulling their back leg through as quickly as they can to take their first race stride. A sprinter's first stride is the shortest they take in a race, measuring around 1 metre. For the next 20 to 30 metres, sprinters continue to drive forward, powerfully assisted by a vigorous arm action. The arms pump back and forth, not across their body, with the elbows passing close to their sides. Their body is held low and their head is held down, with their eyes focused on the track a few metres ahead.

Acceleration

After leaving the starting blocks, the sprinter increases their running speed in what is known as the pick-up or acceleration phase. Speed in sprinting is often called horizontal velocity – the rate at which a sprinter covers the ground ahead of them. It is measured by multiplying the length of an athlete's stride by their cadence (stride rate). Sprinters accelerate by increasing both their stride length and their cadence, still leaning forward as they power ahead. During the acceleration phase, male sprinters make up to 4.6 strides per second while female sprinters reach up to 4.4 or 4.5 strides per second.

This sequence of photographs shows the drive out of the blocks and into the acceleration phase. The sprinter's body straightens up and his strides get progressively longer as he heads into his full sprinting action.

Sprinters need excellent balance to stay in their lane as they power off from their starting blocks. American athlete Gwen Torrance was distraught after being disqualified for running out of her lane in the 200m at the 1995 World Championships.

Running the 200m

The 200m sprint makes extra demands on athletes. As well as being further than the 100m, the runners have to run round a bend as well as finishing on the straight. The start lines for the lanes are **staggered** so that each competitor has the same distance to run. For example, the starting line for lane 6 is 3.83 metres ahead of lane 5's starting line.

French athlete Marie-Jose Perec shows how 200m sprinters lean inwards and press their left shoulder forward as they run the bend.

Running the bend

Sprinters have to work hard on their bend-running technique. Stepping onto the lines or into the next lane means they will be **disqualified**. Running a bend at top speed pushes 200m sprinters to the outside of their lane. Athletes lean into the bend and press their left shoulder slightly forwards. Some slightly shorten their running stride around a bend. These techniques help keep a runner on the inside of their lane, making their race distance shorter.

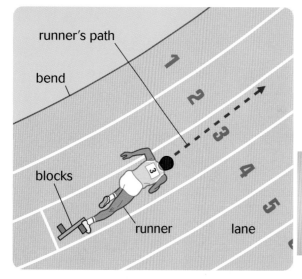

runner's path

bend

blocks

runner

lane

In 200m races, athletes set their starting blocks at an angle to the bend. This is so that they can run their first few strides in a straight line, to produce as much acceleration as possible.

Two-phase race

As the bend ends, sprinters reach the midway point of the race. Now their true race positions are revealed. Even though **fatigue** hits sprinters in the last 50 metres of the race, top-class 200m runners tend to run the second 100 metres between 0.2 and 0.5 seconds faster. This is due to running on the straight and to the flying start they get for the second 100 metres.

Lane fact

At some competitions, lots are drawn for lanes. At others, the fastest qualifiers for a race are given the middle lanes. The outside lane (8) has the most gentle curve. The inside lanes (1 and 2) are a tighter curve but sprinters can see how fast the competitors ahead of them are running. Most sprinters prefer lanes 3, 4 or 5.

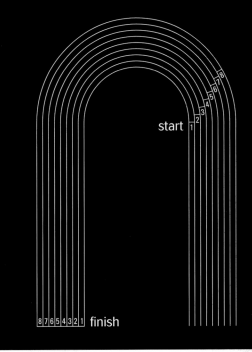

start

8 7 6 5 4 3 2 1 finish

Johnson wins gold!

American sprinter Michael Johnson dominated both 200m and 400m racing throughout the 1990s. A brilliant bend runner, Johnson had an unusual, upright, short-striding running style. He won five Olympic gold medals. In 1996 he shattered the 200m world record with a time of 19.32 seconds.

Maintaining speed and fighting fatigue

Top sprinters reach their maximum speed a little over halfway through a race. The target then is to maintain this pace for as long as possible, as well as to minimize how much deceleration or slowing down occurs close to the finishing line.

A sprinter's leg presses down and back onto the track with the rest of the athlete ahead of their foot on impact. The reaction of this pushing force moves the sprinter forwards and upwards.

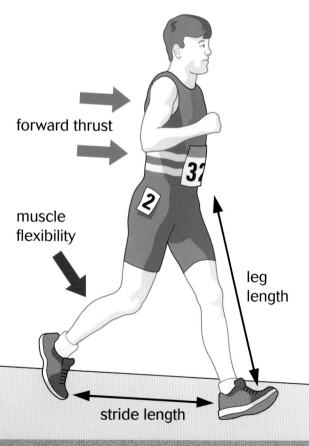

forward thrust

muscle flexibility

leg length

stride length

The maximum speed zone

Champion 100m sprinters usually reach their maximum speed after 60 metres of a race. They only spend between 20 and 30 metres at their top speed, but this period is crucial to their chances of success. Top speeds for elite male athletes are around 12 metres per second – that is equivalent to 43.2 kph, a staggering speed. The best female sprinters are not far behind, reaching around 40 kph.

A sprinter's stride length is determined by the length of their leg, the flexibility of their muscles and how much forward thrust they generate when running.

As champion sprinter Frankie Fredericks (second from left) gets close to the finishing line, he tries to maintain a still upper body with his arms moving smoothly close to his sides.

Staying focused

All top sprinters try to stay focused and keep their body as relaxed as possible, despite the intense effort they are putting in. Tenseness saps energy and can lead to jerkiness in an athlete's movement, which also reduces speed. Sprinters strive to keep their neck, shoulders and hands loose and keep their upper body as still as they can. This improves sprinting speed by helping to transfer as much power as possible to the sprinter's legs.

Deceleration phase

The final 10 to 20 metres of a 100m or 200m race is called the deceleration phase. During this stage of the race, the **fatigue** of performing at maximum effort and speed begins to affect the body's functioning. Stride rates tend to decrease and some sprinters try to compensate by increasing their stride length. The fight to stay running in a relaxed, fluid style is now at its greatest as the finishing line looms.

Tracks and lanes: then and now

Sprinters at the early Olympics had to contend with poorly built and slow tracks. In the case of the 1900 Olympics, there was no actual track, just grass. Lanes were frequently marked out with ropes tied to stakes, as in this photo from the 1924 Olympics. Sprinters veering out of their lane risked tripping over the ropes. In 1928 the stakes were replaced by chalk lines marking out the lanes. Tracks improved and in 1968, faster, synthetic (man-made) track surfaces were used in the Olympics. Today, sprint lanes must be 1.22 metres in width.

A winning finish

Sprinters are at their most tired as they approach the finishing line. To complete a race, the **torso** of a sprinter's body must cross the finishing line. Legs, arms and the head do not count.

Crossing the line

Champion sprinters focus on the finishing line and strive to maintain top speed through and past the finish. In close race situations, some sprinters lunge or dip for the line, throwing their arms back and thrusting their chest forward as they make their last race stride. Timing is essential, as dipping too early or too late can lose a sprinter one or more race places. Coaches emphasize to younger sprinters the importance of not thinking about dipping but instead, running through the line using their normal running style, in order to maintain as much speed as possible.

Wind assistance fact

Headwinds – winds blowing into a runner's face – tend to increase race times while tailwinds can decrease times. A tailwind – blowing from behind a runner – cannot be more than 2.0 metres per second during a race otherwise the times are known as wind-assisted. The race result still stands, as every sprinter on the track was affected in the same way, but a time does not make the record books if it is wind-assisted.

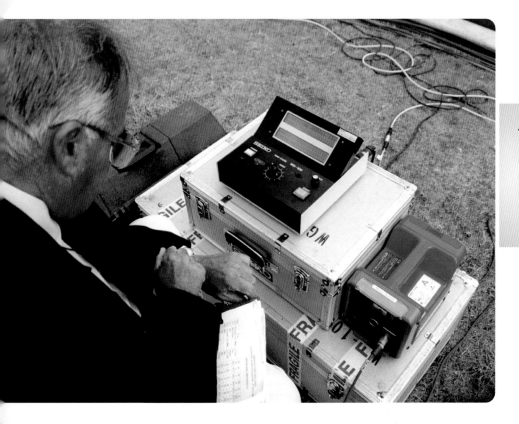

An official studies an electronic wind meter used to measure the speed and direction of wind at track competitions.

Photo-finish

Some sprint finishes are almost too close to call. Track competitions use sophisticated electronics and cameras to provide officials with photographs of the approach to, and crossing of, the line by athletes. This equipment, linked to the starter's gun and the electronic timing system, casts a beam of invisible light across the finishing line. When broken by a runner's body, the sprinter's time is logged. Shortly after a race is completed at a major stadium, the times are displayed on giant screens for the crowd and the athletes to see.

Personal best

Sprinters keep a complete record of their best times in different events and different conditions. Their personal best (PB) or personal record (PR) is the fastest official time they have ever run a particular distance in a recognized competition. Beating their personal best for a distance is always a major target for a sprinter.

The official photo of the 1996 Olympic men's 100m final shows Canadian sprinter Donovan Bailey's chest (far right) breaking the finishing line first. Bailey's time of 9.84 seconds was also a new world record.

Too close to call!

Better known as a 110m hurdler, American Gail Devers has starred in a number of exciting 100m races. At the 1993 World Championships, Devers and Jamaican athlete Merlene Ottey recorded exactly the same time of 10.82. After studying the finish photos, the officials decided that Devers (in lane 5) had crossed the line fractionally ahead of Ottey and declared her the winner.

Training for speed

Sprinters go through hundreds of hours of training every year in order to improve their race times. A large range of training techniques is used, because sprinting has many different aspects to it. Key parts of sprint training concentrate on improving an athlete's flexibility, endurance, speed, strength and power.

Two sprinters perform speedwork exercises on a track, urged on by British ex-Olympic 100m champion, Linford Christie.

Increasing stride length

As we have seen, a runner's speed is the length of their stride multiplied by how many strides he or she makes in a second. Flexibility and strength are worked on together in order to increase an athlete's stride length without sacrificing their speed of movement. The improvements may often sound small, a matter of one or two centimetres. However, as a sprinter takes over 40 strides in a 100m race, this can add up to a vital half metre that might separate the winner from the rest.

Speedwork

Speedwork aims to improve how fast a sprinter's muscles can work to help increase the stride rate. There are many different forms of exercises in speedwork. A common exercise involves running sets of short sprints at almost full speed, with short rest-periods in between sets. For example, a sprinter may run four or five 40m sprints at around 90 per cent speed, with a 3-minute recovery period before they perform another set of four. The idea of this sort of exercise is to condition the muscles to work at a faster rate.

Sprint loading

Sprint loading is one well-known method of improving speed and acceleration. Weights or some other sort of resistance are added to an athlete's body while they are sprinting. The planned effect is to get a sprinter's body to create more force to overcome the weight or resistance and still move at the same speed. A vest that can be fitted with a series of light weights is one commonly used method. A small parachute attached to a sprinter via a harness is another.

Gluteus maximus

Quadriceps

Hamstrings

Adductor

Iliotibial tract

Peroneus

Gastrocnemius

Soleus

Muscles are arranged around the body in a series of muscle groups. Many of the major leg muscles used in sprinting are labelled here.

This athlete is being towed along by a harness attached to a car. Called overspeed training, it forces the athlete's legs and body to work more quickly than if they were running by themselves. This sort of training is dangerous and should only ever be undertaken by a professional!

Explosive power!

Sprinters need to explode out of their **starting blocks** and into a race. They need a combination of great strength and rapid movement, which together are known as explosive power.

Top sprinters spend a lot of time in the gym, especially during the off-season months before major competitions. Here, a sprinter performs a chest press exercise to strengthen muscles in his upper body.

Strength and power

A sprinter's foot is only in contact with the track for less than a tenth of a second when running flat out. During this time, the sprinter has to produce as much force as possible to propel themselves forward. Power is the ability to exert force quickly. This is especially important at the start of a race, where sprinters need to accelerate from zero to over 40 kph in around six seconds.

By building power, a sprinter is often able to increase their stride rate and stride length, enabling them to achieve faster race times.

This athlete is using a resistance-training technique that has been popular with a number of sprinters, including Marita Koch, Evelyn Ashford and Linford Christie. The parachute adds resistance to the athlete's movements, forcing his body to use greater force to overcome the slowing effects of the parachute. Muscle strength can build as a result.

Warming up

All training sessions, whether they are to work on speed or power work, begin with a period of warm-up activity involving a series of muscle stretches, running and other movements. Warming up is vital in many ways, as it prepares the body for the training session ahead. It gradually increases the workload on the sprinter's heart and lungs. It also increases body temperature and warms muscles, which helps to improve their flexibility. A more flexible muscle group is one less likely to be torn or strained during exercise.

Ligaments and tendons fact

Ligaments are bands of tough, fibrous tissue that hold bones together, particularly at the joints. Tendons are connective tissues that join muscles to bones. Warming up well helps reduce the chances of either tendons or ligaments suffering damage.

Plyometrics

Athletes build strength and power using many different training techniques, including weights sessions in the gym. One popular form of power training is called **plyometrics**.

Muscles contract fastest when they have just been stretched. For example, dropping down into a crouched position then immediately springing upwards will result in a higher jump than from a standing start. By pre-stretching a muscle tightly and then quickly contracting it, plyometric drills enable muscles to build to reach maximum strength in a relatively short time. The additional muscle strength helps the sprinters generate more forward speed as they run. Many plyometrics exercises involve bounding, jumping or hopping using great effort.

Here, Christine Arron of France is practising her starting technique. The faster a sprinter can explode out of the starting blocks, the better!

Building endurance

A sprint race may be over in a matter of seconds, but top sprinters still need to work on their endurance levels. In sprinting, endurance means being able to maintain maximum pace in a race for as long as possible.

Winter training

Much of a sprinter's endurance training takes place in the winter, months before the start of the major competitions. Some sprinters may look to build general fitness and endurance by running a series of longer distances or by cross-training – exercising using other sports. All sprinters, however, build speed endurance using **interval training**.

Interval training

Interval training is similar to speedwork (see page 22). It aims to improve the heart, lungs and circulatory system's ability to transport oxygen around the body. Interval training exercises vary. They tend to involve a series of short runs at close to maximum effort followed by a short rest. These series of runs are repeated in sets so that a sprinter has to sprint again before being fully recovered.

Coaches and their sprinters work on different interval training exercises. A typical exercise may see a sprinter run five sets of four 70m sprints at 90 per cent of their maximum effort. Between each set, there may be a three-minute period of rest and recovery before another set is run.

Sprinters have to train in the winter. Warm clothing is essential, especially for the break (interval) between training runs. If a sprinter doesn't keep warm, their muscles lose flexibility, making a muscle strain or injury more likely.

VO2 max

Top sprinters' endurance levels are tested regularly. One of the most common endurance measures is called VO2 max, which is short for Maximum Oxygen Uptake Capacity. This is the amount of oxygen a person's cells can absorb in one minute while working at their full capacity. A higher VO2 max means a runner can absorb more oxygen in a given time and is likely to be able to train harder and run faster.

Sprinters undergo a range of tests to monitor their fitness and endurance levels. They use the results to modify their training programmes.

Who won gold in this 100m race at the 1991 World Championships in Tokyo? Carl Lewis, the runner on the far left of the picture. All sprinters lose speed as they come to the end of a race. A sprinter who appears to finish faster or comes from behind to win a race is simply one who slows down less than the others. Lewis was renowned for his 'fast finish'.

Anaerobic energy pathways fact

Energy pathways are the different ways a body produces energy to contract its muscles. Sprinting with maximum effort is an **anaerobic** activity, which means without oxygen. When sprinting, the body is working so hard that the demands for oxygen are greater than the athlete can supply. When oxygen supplies are limited, the muscles rely instead on stored reserves of fuel. Endurance training for sprinters works on improving anaerobic energy efficiency.

Diet and nutrition

Every champion sprinter takes what they eat and drink extremely seriously. Sprinters and their coaches consult with experts in diet and nutrition to prepare meals that give the athlete the best possible chance of success.

Proteins are a series of substances which are essential in building and repairing many parts of the body including muscles, bones, skin and internal organs. Sprinters eat a lot of protein-rich foods in their diet from food sources such as lean meat, fish, chicken and pulses such as lentils.

Low-fat diet

Food does not only provide sprinters with the energy their muscles need to run fast. It also provides energy and nutrients that keep all the body systems working and help to repair damage. Healthy diets provide people with quantities of seven essential groups of substances: vitamins, minerals, fibre, water, proteins, fats and carbohydrates. Fats are stored inside the human body where they act as a reserve energy store and help keep people warm whilst protecting vital organs. Sprinters, however, require low levels of body fat while being strong and muscular. As a result, sprinters try to eat a diet that contains foods rich in nutrients, which will enable their bodies to recover from long periods of training. Foods which contain high levels of fat, such as deep-fried foods, are kept to a minimum in their diet.

Carbohydrates and glycogen

Carbohydrates are a range of different substances found in many foods including fresh fruit and vegetables, porridge, pasta and rice. Carbohydrates provide much of the energy required for intense activity such as sprinting. Some carbohydrate energy is stored in the liver and muscles in the form of the substance glycogen.

When in training, most elite sprinters eat a diet that is rich in carbohydrates, helping their body to store more glycogen. Studies have shown that muscles are better able to retain carbohydrate during the two hours after a long exercise period. Sprinters often consume their largest meal of the day in this period at the end of training.

Topping up

Water is lost from the body in many ways, including through sweating and through the air we breathe out. While a 10-second sprint will not cause a major loss of water from the body, **dehydration** can occur during long periods of training or on a competition day that involves a number of races. A lack of water in the body can greatly hamper an athlete's performance, so sprinters are careful to top up their fluid levels throughout the day.

US sprinter Marion Jones relaxes with a sports drink in hand after running the women's 200m qualifier at the 2001 World Championships. Sprinters involved in a long day of training or competition try to restore glycogen levels between events by eating a small snack or having a sports drink rich in carbohydrates.

Maurice Greene

When the USA's Maurice Greene started to take sprinting seriously, he turned his back on eating lots of fried and fatty foods and started to eat a healthy diet suitable for sprinting. Greene said: 'Diet is very important. You put out so much energy, that you have to make sure you're putting it back into your body. I eat a lot of chicken and fish, vegetables and baked foods. I eat three times a day plus I also take multi-vitamins.'

Injuries and recovery

Sprinters push their bodies to the limit in order to race at incredible speeds. They run right at the edge of the human body's capacity and, as a result, injuries are common. A major injury is a sprinter's worst nightmare.

Muscle stresses and strains

Many sprinters suffer injuries at some point in their career. Lower back muscles and leg muscles such as the **hamstring** and calf are the ones most likely to suffer soreness, strains or, even worse, tears in the muscle fibres. While some injuries may require surgery, the best treatment for most injuries suffered by sprinters is rest. The injured body part needs time to heal.

In recovery

Top-flight sprinters have to be patient during the recovery phase. Returning to full training or competition racing too soon can make an injury far worse. When recovering from an injury, sprinters train gently to keep as much of their general fitness levels and suppleness as possible without placing too much strain on the injured part of their body. For example, during the recovery phase, a sprinter is unlikely to perform heavy weights exercises to build explosive power.

Throughout the recovery period, a sprinter's coach and doctor carefully monitor their condition. A long injury, proving slow to heal, may require operations and visits to many medical specialists.

Two British sprinters suffered injuries in the 2002 Commonwealth Games 100m final. Dwain Chambers (left) suffered from a leg cramp while Mark Lewis-Francis (right) suffered a small tear in his hamstring muscle on his right leg.

Aqua training

Sprinters recovering from some muscle and ligament injuries often resort to swimming and special exercises in water known as aqua training. The aquajogger is one popular form of aqua training. It is a foam belt strapped around the waist that keeps the sprinter's body afloat and lets them perform a running motion in water without the stresses and impact of their feet hitting a solid surface. Exercising in water allows the arms and legs to move freely with equal resistance working a large number of the different muscle groups.

Trinidad and Tobago sprinter Ato Boldon lies on the track and receives a massage during a practice session at the Sydney Olympics, 2000.

A triumphant return

Namibian sprinter Frankie Fredericks withdrew from the 2000 Sydney Olympics with an ankle injury, underwent two operations and spent almost two years out of racing. Many feared that Fredericks, in his thirties, would never return to the track. In 2002, he not only made the final of the Commonwealth Games 200m, but won in 20.06 seconds. Emotional afterwards, he said: 'I went through so much trouble. I feared I might be finished. This is one of the medals I will never forget.'

Drugs and drugs testing

One of the most controversial aspects of modern athletics is drug-taking and testing. Drugs are chemical substances that have an effect on the human body. A number of drugs, whether they are legal or illegal in society, are banned from sports. This is because, as well as being dangerous, they could give athletes that use them an unfair advantage over their fellow competitors.

Doping

Despite these bans, the pressure of competing to be the best, along with the influences of coaches and officials, has led some top sprinters into doping – the use of forbidden substances in order to enhance their performance. Doping is considered cheating just like breaking any other rule in athletics. It can seriously affect the health of a sportsperson and has, in a number of cases, resulted in an early and painful death. Doping also damages the image of sprinters as role models to young people.

Anabolic steroids

Anabolic steroids are the class of banned substance most closely associated with sprinting and other explosive power sports such as weightlifting. Steroids can spur large amounts of muscle growth, enabling sprinters to train harder and longer. Their side-effects are many and serious. For example, they can permanently harm the liver, kidneys and heart, can make people very aggressive and can cause a number of physical changes in the bodies of people who take them.

Thousands of different drugs exist, a number of which are on the International Olympic Committee's list of banned substances. This is divided into types or classes of drug. The drugs in this picture are anabolic steroids.

Modern drugs testing

Drugs testing was first introduced at the 1968 Mexico Olympics but it was not until the 1980s that testing became rigorous and frequent. Drugs testing is performed by national authorities and also by officials at international athletics events. Drugs-testing officials can also perform out-of-competition testing – arriving, for example, at a sprinter's training camp. Tests often involve taking a urine sample, which is divided in two and stored in separate containers to avoid contamination. The two samples are sent to a laboratory and, if both samples test positive for a banned drug, a process of appeals and hearings takes place.

A technical officer at work in the Australian sports drug testing laboratory in Sydney. At the 2000 Olympics, 2758 drugs tests were carried out.

Sanctions

If a sprinter fails a drugs test, they are usually sent home from the competition they are attending. If their appeal fails and they are found guilty of doping, serious punishments, called sanctions, await them. In Olympic competition, this now means a two-year ban if it is a sprinter's first offence. A second offence carries a life ban.

Ben Johnson

In 1988, Canadian sprinter Ben Johnson recorded a time of 9.79 seconds to win the 100m Olympics final, smashing the world record in the process. Within days, he was found to have tested positive for a performance-enhancing steroid called stanozol. Johnson was stripped of his gold medal and world record and banned from competing for two years. In 1993, when he tested positive again, Johnson was banned from international competitions for life.

Peaking to perfection

Elite sprinters train almost all year round. However, sprinters and their coaches tailor training so that athletes are at their best as the major races of the season approach.

Training calendar

The end of the outdoor season is followed by a short rest and holiday period and then the off season, when few major races take place. During this time, sprinters train hard in the gym to increase their strength, explosive power and flexibility. Coaches and sprinters also work closely to improve other skills needed, such as sprinting with a steady upper body (which helps a sprinter generate more forward speed). As the competitive season approaches, sprinters tend to train more on the track, with speed drills and **interval training** to increase their pace.

Tapering *fact*

Tapering is the easing down of training in the days and weeks before a major competition. Training doesn't stop, but the workouts the sprinter performs often lessen in number and intensity. Heavy training greatly tires muscles. The aim of tapering is to give muscles time to rest and recover before a major competition so that they can perform at their very best.

Many elite sprinters have their training and drill times measured accurately using electronic equipment. The Swift Speedlight equipment shown here can measure an athete's times down to a hundredth of a second.

The indoor season

Early in the year, many sprinters take part in the indoor track season held in indoor stadiums sheltered from the weather. Some sprinters specialize in indoor sprints. Most, though, use it as a way of working on track speed and sharpening their racing reactions prior to the outdoor season later in the year. Indoor sprints are run on two tracks. The 60m replaces the 100m as the shortest sprint and is usually run on a straight track often inside the indoor arena's oval track. The oval track is 200 metres long and has banked curves. This means that the outer lanes are higher from the floor than the inside lanes. Almost all sprinters prefer the outer lanes, as the bends on the inside lanes are extremely tight.

Marcia Richardson (front left) wins a 60m indoor race in 2001. The previous year, she was selected for the Great Britain team to run the 100m at the 2000 Sydney Olympics.

Trials and tribulations

Some nations, including the USA, pick their team for the Olympics and other major championships using events called **trials**. The top three finishers in each athletics event earn a place in the US team, providing they have run inside times set by the Olympics as qualifying standards. In the 2000 US Olympic trials, the contest between Maurice Greene (right) and Michael Johnson (left) in the 200m was eagerly awaited. However, both men limped out halfway through the final with injuries. Neither was selected to run in the Olympics at 200m, although they would both have been favourites for medals.

The major competitions

There are dozens of top athletics meetings held all over the world. Some occur every year while others are held every two or four years. Sprinters choose to attend a number of events in the racing season. But they plan and time their training so that they peak for their biggest target of the year – usually one of the major competitions, such as the Olympics or the World Championships.

The Olympics

The summer Olympics, held every four years, is the biggest single sporting event in the world, attracting over 10,000 competitors from more than 190 nations. Sprint finals at the Olympics are watched by tens of thousands of live spectators and TV audiences measured in hundreds of millions. The 2000 games were held in Sydney, Australia, the 2004 games in Athens, Greece whilst in 2008, the games are set to be staged in China's capital city of Beijing.

Olympics fact

The first modern Olympic Games were held in 1896 in the Greek city of Athens and featured athletes from just 14 countries. Of the 245 competitors who attended, 164 were Greek. The winner of the 100m final, however, was the USA's Thomas Burke. He ran the distance in a time of 12.0 seconds.

Athletes from all the competing national teams gathered around the running track during the opening ceremony of the 2000 Olympic Games in Sydney, Australia.

World Championships

The first World Championships were held in 1983 in Helsinki, Finland. The first three Championships took place four years apart. Since that time, the competition has been held every two years in Europe, Japan and Canada. The ninth World Championships were held in Paris, France in August 2003. The expected 100m showdown between the US and British sprinters did not materialize, as Kim Collins of St Kitts & Nevis took gold with a time of 10.07. There was greater success for the USA, however, in the men's 200m and the women's 100m, which were won by John Capel and Torri Edwards respectively.

Jesse Owens, sprinting legend

One of the most legendary series of performances by a sprinter at a major championships occurred at the 1936 Olympics held in Berlin, Germany. American sprinter Jesse Owens stunned spectators by scooping four gold medals. He won the 100m in 10.3 seconds, the long jump, the 200m in 20.7 seconds and was part of the US 4 x 100m relay team that won gold and broke the world record with a time of 39.8 seconds.

Regional competitions

Major competitions exist for different parts of the world and only sprinters from the countries of that region can attend. The European Championships were first held in 1934 and attract sprinters from more than 30 countries. The Pan-American Games were first held in 1951 and are held once every four years in the year before the Summer Olympics. They are open to athletes from the nations of both North and South America.

World Indoor Championships

The first World Indoor Championships were held in 1987 in the US city of Indianapolis. The eighth Championships were held in Birmingham, UK, in March 2003 and saw 650 competitors from over 140 different nations take part. Ukrainian Zhanna Block won the women's 60m while Justin Gatlin from the USA took the men's 60m title in 6.46 seconds.

A series of races

In many competitions, sprinters and other athletes enter as individuals. But in international competitions such as the Olympic Games and the World Championships, athletes go as part of a national team. Sprinters have to work towards these events knowing they will need to run more than one fast race to triumph.

Qualifying to go

Each country is usually allowed to enter only three athletes into an event. Many nations, including the USA, use **trials** to select the national team (see page 35). Others, such as the UK, use trials but also reserve further places for outstanding athletes who may not have succeeded at the trials.

Making the last eight

Dozens of sprint competitors arrive at an Olympics or World Championships with the aim of winning their event. Many will be disappointed, as only eight competitors can line up in the final that will determine the winner. Athletes take part in races known as **heats** or rounds, in which the first two or three to finish in each heat qualify for the next stage. At some competitions, some of the **fastest losers** from the heats go through as well.

As the field narrows down to semi-finals, nerves start to get exposed. If athletes get any part of their race wrong, they may not make it into the four that reach the final to face the fastest four from the other semi-final. The men's 100m semi-finals at the 2003 World Championships saw such notable athletes as Ato Bolden and Mark Lewis-Francis fail to make the final.

US sprinter Dennis Mitchell performs an arm and shoulder stretch during his warm-up routine. Most sprinters try to warm up relatively vigorously between 45–60 minutes before race time.

Relays

Some 100m and 200m sprinters are selected to run in a team sprinting event known as a relay. There are two relay distances – the 4 x 100m and the 4 x 400m. Both involve four sprinters running a 100m or 400m section, or leg, of the race. The first three runners have to pass a baton to the next runner at the end of their leg of the race. Baton-changing at high speed can be difficult and relay racing calls for much practice between teammates. Some sprinters choose not to enter the event so that they can concentrate on their individual sprints.

Baton fact

In relays, runners must exchange the baton within the 20-metre-long take-over zone and stay in their lane until all the exchanges have been made. An athlete who drops the baton can pick it up again and run on, but they will have lost so much time they have little hope of winning the race.

US 4 x 100m relay runner Jason Smoots sweeps his arm upwards to pass the baton into the outstretched hand of team-mate Kaaron Conwright at the 2002 World Cup competition in Spain. The US team went on to win the race.

Doubling up

The technique and extreme pace required for the 100m and 200m sprints are similar. Some athletes choose to enter both races at a championships. This is known as doubling up. To win the sprint double is a massive test of fitness and resolve because the competitors have to run as many as eight races over just a few days. Only a handful of sprinters have ever managed to win the sprint double at the Olympics. These include the Soviet athlete Valeriy Borzov in 1972 and Americans Carl Lewis in 1984 and Marion Jones in 2000.

Before and after a race

Top sprinters and their coaches work back from the start time of a race to develop their own unique timetable in the hours and minutes leading up to an event. Once out on the track, however, a sprinter is alone and needs strong powers of concentration in order to race well.

Their own routine

Every sprinter has their own **regime** on race day. For example, when and what a sprinter eats is carefully thought through with their coach and depends on how many races a sprinter has to face. Many sprinters' pre-race regimes are closely guarded secrets. Out in the stadium and stripped of their tracksuits, every sprinter has their own well-drilled routine before they get into their **starting blocks**. Nearly all sprinters, for example, perform some final, gentle stretches and make a short series of practice starts.

Thinking tough

An Olympic 100m gold medallist, former 100m world record holder and World Champion at both 100m and 200m, Maurice Greene firmly believes in having a tough mental approach to sprinting. 'When the gun fires you must concentrate for every second on the way to that finish line. You should know exactly how long it will take you… and think about every step of the race you are about to run.'

Lane placing fact

In outdoor sprints and the indoor 60m, the fastest four athletes are placed in the four middle lanes so that the favourites to win are grouped together. In the indoor 200m, the outer lanes are usually given to the fastest sprinters so that they have a less tight bend to run. In **heats**, the qualification or entry time (often the sprinter's best time for the season) is used to determine fastest and slowest. In later rounds, the times in the previous rounds are used to sort lane placings.

Mental focus

For young sprinters, entering a major championship stadium for the first time can be an intimidating experience. They can find themselves surveying the stadium, crowd or their rivals and getting tense with nerves as a result. Champion sprinters tend to be mentally very strong. Linford Christie, for example, was renowned for his ability to stay relaxed and focused both before and during a race.

US sprinters Coby Miller and John Capel console each other after coming seventh and eighth in the Sydney Olympics 200m final. Losing is tough, but for the very best sprinters, it fuels their desire to train harder and run faster in future.

After the race

A short time after each race, all competitors warm down, drink some fluids, get back into warm clothing and usually consult with their coach. For a sprinter completing the final race of a competition, there is also the prospect of meeting family and friends. Before that point, however, there are often media duties to perform. Sprinters are often interviewed trackside or in media centres inside the stadium. Sometimes, the interviews take place before the sprinter has been able to rest and consider their performance and how the race went in detail. It is a far easier task for a winner to give an interview after a lap of honour than it is for those they have beaten to the line!

Being a modern sprint champion

Being a top sprinter is a challenging but rewarding job. Champion sprinters are amongst the most recognized figures in athletics, and amongst the very best paid. Even so, sprinting at the highest level makes great demands on an athlete's time, energy and emotions outside of training and racing.

Within moments of crossing the line in a 60m indoor race in Birmingham, UK, British sprinter Jason Gardener is interviewed for television.

A full-time job

Champion sprinters are full-time professional athletes who train all year round. Even when not in full training, sprinters tend to keep themselves in good condition, watching what they eat and drink.

To compete at the highest level, sprinters have to travel all over the world. Sometimes, they must make trips to medical or training specialists in another country. Much of their training may be conducted at special camps long distances away from their home. Ato Boldon, for example, is from the Caribbean but trains in the USA. In 1998, he ran in nineteen major sprint competitions in Europe, south-east Asia and the Far East.

The rewards of winning

Glory, celebrity, fame and wealth all come to the very best sprinters in today's sport. There may be no prize money for winning the 100m or 200m at the Olympics, but other competitions do offer prizes worth thousands of pounds to sprint finalists and winners. Many competitions also pay appearance fees for the top 100m and 200m stars to attend, whether they win or not. Most top sprinters are sponsored by sportswear and other companies. In addition, they are often paid large sums to endorse all sorts of products, from breakfast cereals to computer games.

Always on duty

Although championship athletics can bring fame and fortune, there are also great pressures. Like many major celebrities, there are constant demands on a champion sprinter's time from fans, sponsors and the media. The very best sprinters have little privacy yet must always remain on their best behaviour. As British sprinter Linford Christie stated: 'There are times when I want to be off-duty and there are times when I might not be in the mood, but I will always sign an autograph or whatever. At the end of the day, it is all the public can get from you. It's not too much to ask.'

Putting something back

Many sprinters try to put something back into the sport that they have become a champion in. Some, like Olympic gold medallist Marion Jones (pictured here signing autographs), have started foundations to raise money for children's charities. Jones has also helped promote the Right To Play charity, which uses sport to improve children's lives in many less developed countries.

World records

To break a world record means a great deal to many sprinters. It tells the world that they have run faster than all their rivals and faster than the great sprinters of the past. As training, diet, tracks and equipment have improved, world record times have got faster and faster. Below are some selected world records over the years in men's and women's 100m, 200m and 4 x 100m races.

Adult male 100m world record			
Athlete (nationality)	Time (seconds)	Year	Place
Tim Montgomery (USA)	9.78	2002	Paris, France
Maurice Greene (USA)	9.79	1999	Athens, Greece
Donovan Bailey (Canada)	9.84	1996	Atlanta, USA
Leroy Burrell (USA)	9.85	1994	Lausanne, Switzerland
Carl Lewis (USA)	9.86	1991	Tokyo, Japan
Leroy Burrell (USA)	9.90	1991	New York, USA
Jim Hines (USA)	9.95	1968	Mexico City, Mexico
Armin Hary (West Germany)	10.0	1960	Zurich, Switzerland
Jesse Owens (USA)	10.2	1936	Chicago, USA
Percy Williams (Canada)	10.3	1930	Toronto, Canada
Donald Lippincott (USA)	10.6	1912	Stockholm, Sweden
Thomas Burke (USA)	12.0	1896	Athens, Greece

Adult female 100m world record			
Athlete (nationality)	Time (seconds)	Year	Place
Florence Griffith Joyner (USA)	10.49	1988	Indianapolis, USA
Evelyn Ashford (USA)	10.76	1984	Zurich, Switzerland
Marlies Oelsner-Goer (East Germany)	10.88	1977	Dresden, East Germany
Annegret Richter (West Germany)	11.01	1976	Montreal, Canada
Wilma Rudolph (USA)	11.2	1961	Stuttgart, West Germany
Shirley Strickland (Australia)	11.3	1955	Warsaw, Poland
Marjorie Jackson (Australia)	11.4	1952	Gifu, Japan
Fanny Blankers-Koen (Netherlands)	11.5	1948	Amsterdam, Netherlands
Stanislawa Walasiewicz (Poland)	11.6	1937	Berlin, Germany
Tollien Schuurman (Netherlands)	11.9	1932	Haarlem, Netherlands
Mary Lines (UK)	12.8	1922	Paris, France
Marie Mejzlíková (Czechoslovakia)	13.6	1922	Prague, Czechoslovakia

Adult male 200m world record			
Athlete (nationality)	Time (seconds)	Year	Place
Michael Johnson (USA)	19.32	1996	Atlanta, USA
Michael Johnson (USA)	19.66	1996	Atlanta, USA
Pietro Mennea (Italy)	19.72	1979	Mexico City, Mexico
Tommie Smith (USA)	19.83	1968	Mexico City, Mexico
Tommie Smith (USA)	20.0*	1966	Sacramento, USA
Henry Carr (USA)	20.2*	1964	Tempe, USA
Peter Radford (UK)	20.5*	1960	Wolverhampton, UK
Andy Stanfield (USA)	20.6*	1951	Philadelphia, USA
Jesse Owens (USA)	20.7	1936	Berlin, Germany
Helmut Körnig (Germany)	21.0	1928	Bochum, Germany

Adult female 200m world record

Athlete (nationality)	Time (seconds)	Year	Place
Florence Griffith Joyner (USA)	21.34	1988	Seoul, Korea
Florence Griffith Joyner (USA)	21.56	1988	Seoul, Korea
Marita Koch (East Germany)	21.71	1979	Karl-Marx-Stadt, East Germany
Irena Szewinska (Poland)	22.5	1968	Mexico City, Mexico
Wilma Rudolph (USA)	22.9	1960	Corpus Christi, USA
Betty Cuthbert (Australia)	23.2	1956	Sydney, Australia
Stanislawa Walasiewicz (Poland)	23.6	1935	Warsaw, Poland
Kinue Hitomi (Japan)	24.7*	1929	Miyoshima, Japan
Eileen Edwards (UK)	26.0	1926	Paris, France
Marie Mejzlíková (Czechoslovakia)	28.6	1922	Paris, France

Male 4 x 100m relay current world record (last updated September 2003)

Athletes (nationality)	Time (seconds)	Year	Place
Jon Drummond, Andre Cason, Dennis Mitchell, Leroy Burrell (USA)	37.40	1993	Stuttgart, Germany
Michael Marsh, Leroy Burrell, Dennis Mitchell, Carl Lewis (USA)	37.40	1992	Barcelona, Spain

Female 4 x 100m relay current world record (last updated September 2003)

Athletes (nationality)	Time (seconds)	Year	Place
Silke Gladisch, Sabine Rieger, Ingrid Auerswald, Marlies Göhr (East Germany)	41.37	1985	Canberra, Australia

World junior records (athletes 20 years old or under)

Event	Athletes (nationality)	Time (seconds)	Year	Place
100m male	Darrel Brown (Trinidad)	10.01	2003	Paris, France
200m male	Roy Martin (USA)	20.13	1985	Indianapolis, USA
100m female	Katrin Krabbe (East Germany)	10.89	1988	East Berlin, East Germany
200m female	Allyson Felix (USA)	22.11	2003	Mexico City, Mexico

* Indicates races run over 220 yards (201.17 m).

The records on these pages were correct as of 1/12/2003.

Timing of records fact

Sprint races started to be timed accurately from the beginning of the 20th century onwards. At first, times were rounded up to the nearest second or half second. Many early sprints were run over distances measured in yards, but races in metres soon became the standard. From 1977, only metric distances were considered as world records. In the same year, automatic timing to one-hundredth of a second became the only way world records were recorded.

Glossary

anaerobic
activity that uses fuel stored in the body's muscles without using oxygen

Commonwealth Games
a major international championship open to athletes of nations that are part of the Commonwealth, such as the UK, Canada and Australia. It is usually held once every four years.

dehydration
a reduction in the amount of water in the body

disqualified
the exclusion of an athlete from a race or, if it has already been run, the removal of an athlete's place and time from the race records

fastest loser
the sprinter who records the fastest time amongst all those athletes who did not secure an automatic place in the next round of a competition

fatigue
tiredness after doing an activity

hamstring
the large muscles located at the back of the upper leg

heat
an early race of an event, with the top finishers advancing to the semi-finals or finals of the competition

International Olympic Committee
the organization that runs the summer and winter Olympic Games

interval training
a series of runs carried out with maximum effort, separated by short periods of easier running

physiotherapist
a person who treats injuries and health problems using massage, exercises and heat

physique
the shape of someone's body

plyometrics
a form of intense training exercise which helps build power

reaction time
the time it takes for a sprinter to react to the starter's gun

regime
a systematic way of doing something

sponsorship
money from private companies used to promote sports or sportspeople

staggered
spread out and not in a line

stamina
the ability to keep performing at close to maximum effort for a period of time

starting blocks
a pair of angled supports for the feet, used to increase the power of a sprinter from a crouch start

torso
the body of a person, but not their arms, legs or head

trials
races to decide which athletes will represent their country at a major competition

World Cup
a competition featuring teams from continents as well as individual nations

Resources

Further reading

Marion Jones: Sprinting Sensation, Mark Stewart (Children's Press, 2000).

A biography of top US sprinter Marion Jones.

Sprinting and Hurdling, Peter Warden (The Crowood Press, 1989).

An in-depth look at many of the techniques, exercises and drills used by sprinters to improve their speed, stamina and race sharpness.

The Sprints, Morgan Hughes (Rourke Publishing Group, 2001).

A guide to the training, nutrition and techniques used to enable sprinters to compete at their very best.

Top 10 American Men Sprinters, Ron Knapp (Enslow Publishers, 1999).

Profiles of the lives and achievements of some of the world's finest sprint champions.

Top 10 American Women Sprinters, Arlene Bourgeois Molzahn (Enslow Publishers, 1998).

A companion title to the above looking at America's most successful female sprinters.

Websites

http://www.iaaf.org – the website of the International Association of Athletics Federations (IAAF), the world body that runs athletics.

http://www.olympic.org – the home page of the International Olympic movement. The website is full of features and profiles of top sprinters and other athletes.

http://www.wada-ama.org – the home on the Internet of the World Anti-Doping Agency (WADA). The website has many features and news stories on drugs testing and banned substances.

http://www.mogreene.com/ – the official website of the 2000 Olympic men's 100m champion, Maurice Greene.

Disclaimer

All the Internet addresses (URLs) given in this book were valid at the time of going to press. However, due to the dynamic nature of the Internet, some addresses may have changed, or sites may have changed or ceased to exist since publication. While the author and Publishers regret any inconvenience this may cause readers, no responsibility for any such changes can be accepted by either the author or the Publishers.

Index